Got Mojo?

6 Secrets of Explosive Business Growth from the Marketers of the Year

Cory Michael Sanchez

and

Ira Rosen

Got Mojo?

Got Mojo?

Table of Contents

Got Mojo?

Introduction

Winning the *Marketer of the Year* Award here through the Phoenix Business Journal was both a humbling and proud moment for us.

We were competing against some very stiff competition, big dogs like U.S. Airways, Avnet and other Fortune 500 companies here in Arizona.

The award was based on creativity, innovation, and effectiveness in helping companies tell their story to create marketing momentum, and dominate their marketplace.

Our strategies resulted in our unlikely victory, and we're going to share a few of them in this book, and how you can use these same tactics in your business and crush it.

This is brand new content that we're excited to share with you because building a seven-figure income by using automated webinars does not have to be a secret reserved for gurus.

You can hit any goal you set out to hit. This system will show you how.

In this book we're going to teach you how to create and make money from your webinar.

No matter what business you're in, whether you're a real estate broker, software developer, lawyer, a CPA, doctor, dentist, pretty much anything, you can learn from this.

Businesses all over the world have tried this and it has been proven to work amazingly well.

You're going to discover the simple math of:

- getting a 97% open rate

- getting up to 80% of your prospects to buy on the first call

You'll also learn about the traffic-stack method so you can send hoards of traffic and prospects into an automated selling appointment-getting machine.

In other words, prepare yourself for some startling, game-changing discoveries that will move your business from Point A to Point B on a much faster trajectory.

So grab a beverage, turn off the phone, sit back and get ready to be excited. It all starts now.

To Your Success,

Ira and Cory

Got Mojo?

Chapter 1

The Back of the Napkin

The best way to start this is at the beginning with the story of Mojo, which really puts things in the right perspective.

The most important thing to us is family. It's the reason we are so passionate about helping entrepreneurs around the world reach their revenue goals. Our mission is to help 1 million entrepreneurs use video in their businesses in powerful ways that gives them the freedom to spend more time with those they care about.

But how did this all start?

It all started with an idea of changing the

world, and the massive action to make this goal a reality.

You see, Ira and I possess the persistence, dedication, and drive to succeed.

It all stems from our days as high-level athletes. Ira was an alternate for the U.S. Olympic team for wrestling and I was a highly-ranked Olympic level gymnast who won a silver medal at nationals. We dedicated our life to succeeding where others thought it was impossible, to reaching new heights of accomplishment that others had only dreamed about.

As a result, Ira and I had quite a bit in common, so we hit it off.

Ira has also accomplished quite a bit, spending millions on advertisements, creating numerous multi-million dollar companies, and figuring out how to outsell, out-hustle and out-think the competition.

Ira was training for marathons when I met him, and has run over a hundred thousand miles over the course of his life, with minimal injuries. If you do the math, that's four times around the earth, which is a clearly insane number.

Naturally, I wanted to know the secrets to success that Ira discovered over the years, so I made the bold decision to train with him. Never having run before, I dedicated myself to training with him so I could absorb his knowledge and wisdom.

We trained for hundreds of hours and I got to know some of the things he knew. I was a sponge. For example, Ira discovered at an early age that if you wanted to sell more stuff, if you want to have more sales, you must have more sales presentations.

It's always been a numbers game. How many people can you get in front of?

He also shared with me that the problem is 90% of most entrepreneurs days' are completely non-revenue producing. Can you relate to this challenge? Pick up the book by Timothy Ferriss, *The 4-Hour Workweek* and you'll be 100% certain of this reality and armed with the determination to change this forever.

I kept learning more and more. Ira and I had quickly developed a powerful win-win relationship. He's helping me with getting big clients.

Got Mojo?

I'm helping him with the Internet marketing side of things. Soon it all came together.

And I know this may sound cliché but it's true — we actually got together one day at a burger joint and wrote a business plan down on the back of the napkin. That is when Mojo was born.

Today we have clients in 22 different countries. We have companies of all shapes and sizes doing business with us, from tire companies to new car dealerships to CPA firms and dental firms and lawyers and speakers and authors and franchises and non-profits and, well, you get the idea.

We've also been able to speak on stage next to the movers and shakers of personal and professional development, people like Mark Victor Hansen, Les Brown and T. Harv Eker.

This is just scratching the surface of what we're all about, but this book is more about you and helping you achieve the runaway success you have always envisioned for yourself and your company.

Chapter 2

Passion + Velocity = Big Time Success

What you must know before we get too far along is this:

When we first started, we had zero clients. We had no revenue, no recurring revenue, no database and very little chance for success.

But we had a dream and a passion, and we were determined to do whatever it took to make that dream a reality. This is what you need to have, and I'm sure you already do. We at Mojo call this W.I.T., which stands for Whatever It Takes!

Of course, for big success to start happening for you it will require a re-invention of your marketing and your message. You will need to keep your message fresh, hot and relevant, since the Internet is such a fast moving medium.

It's all about velocity.

To reach the right velocity in the most consistent and effective way we produce video. Now, believe it or not this wasn't always easy for us. It took us upwards of 20 to 30 takes to do our first video.

So, if you're not doing video because you think the task is too daunting, we have been there, believe me! That's why we're going to show you step-by-step how to use our marketing systems, and we will leave no stone unturned. More than that, we found out how to make it work for virtually any business out there, and how you can use it with your business no matter what your technology level. By the end of this book, you will be armed with how to make this work for you.

Let's face it. Getting clients is tough in this new economy. There are new rules and a whole new game. What used to work in marketing doesn't work anymore. If you think that you can get by without adding a video plan to your marketing arsenal, you may want to re-think that. In fact, right now is the time to push the reset button and <u>re-think everything</u>.

Got Mojo?

Chapter 3

The 6 Secrets

People everywhere are embracing the new economy with new marketing. Ira tells everybody one thing, "Do not let a good recession go to waste. This is an amazing time to do business. This is an amazing time to be an entrepreneur." It's a gold rush right now. When you have massive pain and confusion, you have Massive opportunity, if you have the right marketing. Aside from that, your competition is asleep at the wheel, waiting for something to happen. It's just like going fishing and expecting the fish to jump into your boat!

And we're going to show you why right now, with 6 Secrets to Explosive Business Growth that will shake your foundations to the core.

19

Got Mojo?

Secret #1: Instant Video Follow Up

Networking events are great, but the Achilles' heel of these events is the follow-up. You go home with a pile of business cards and that's it. Very rarely do you make the most of the relationships you develop while at a networking event, or just meeting others while you are about and around.

So to combat this we bring you Secret #1 to our success: **instant video follow-up**. When you meet a prospect you should send them a video follow-up immediately. Every time we went to a networking event or trade show we would do this.

The open rates were phenomenal. The meetings we booked were incredible.

Got Mojo?

And it doesn't just work well for us. It works well for our clients; people like Ray Malnar, an all-stone, tile, and wood restoration expert.

Before he met us, Ray would get calls and he'd travel to give people quotes for woodwork and tile installation. He'd close about 12% of the people that he came in contact with, which wasn't enough. He was struggling and he came to us for help.

We had him do one thing: the video follow-up.

It's just a very simple video, less than 30 seconds. "Hi, I'm Ray. I'm going to be coming out to see your house. Take a look at some of our testimonials and success stories and some examples of our work and I look forward to talking with you soon."

Got Mojo?

He sent that out and his conversion skyrocketed to 50%. Mind you, it didn't go up by 50%; it went up to 50%, which is a 400% increase. To put that into perspective, instead of closing 12 out of 100, he's closing 50 out of a 100.

And this really made a difference to Ray because you can imagine how much he was struggling before he started doing this. This is just one success story. We have many.

So we started looking at the science behind why our systems are working so well.

When you watch a video your brain is in a highly-activated state, filled with feel-good brain chemicals like serotonin, dopamine, and endorphins.

Got Mojo?

Conversely, when you go into check-writing mode, or if you're reading an email, your brain does practically nothing.

Every time they get a video, it's permanently embedded into their conscious and sub-conscious minds.

This is the science of why people love video - because it makes them feel good. One year from now, chances are good that people won't remember what you said to them. What they will remember is how you made them feel. We're talking about relationship marketing on steroids, which is why video is so hot at the moment, and it shows no sign of letting up.

Secret #2: Using SMS Video to get a 97% open rate

Got Mojo?

Sending video emails is just the tip of the iceberg--what about **video text messages**!

When we started sending video text we were pioneers. The way video and mobile marketing has changed in such a short time is just mind-blowing. Think about it: there are six billion phones on this planet and only 2 billion computers.

Everybody is always within a couple feet of their cellular device at all points of the day. But ironically, nobody is actually answering their phone. Therein lays the challenge.

What they are doing is texting, emailing, going on social media, and the list goes on. Everyone's methods of communicating have completely shifted. We are faced with one critical choice: adapt or die!

Got Mojo?

We chose to adapt. We figured out the method for sending video text messages. Combined with our Mojo Matrix video email software, it was a powerful combination.

I hope you're sitting down for this next statistic: Video text messages, in general, get a 97% open rate.

Remember, this is all a numbers game. Since there's more mobile phones on the planet than there are toothbrushes right now (yes, that scary stat is true), and with email open rates at an all time low, this all makes perfect sense.

Bottom line: email is out, video is in. And text message video is right there on the cutting edge. While your competitor's emails are getting deleted, your video text is getting viewed.

Got Mojo?

But there's more great news because we also made a discovery on the follow up side of things. When you follow up your video text with a video email, and even another video text message, results go up even more.

The fact is that 90% of all transactions happen from the 4th to the 12th touch point, 90% of them, and effective follow up is the defining difference between success and failure.

Business is, in a strange way, much like dating. If you go out on a date and you send flowers and notes day after day after day, that person has you on their mind because you're building that relationship.

On the flip side, suppose you have someone who goes on a date and doesn't call the person for a year. But suddenly out of the blue they call this person up and ask him if they want to get married. Guess what happens then...that's right...they get a dial tone.

That's how people are doing business. You have to build solid long term sustainable relation-ships. You must build trust and top of mind awareness that is the cornerstone of all great relationships. At the end of the day it's all about relationship marketing. You see they don't buy because of the product, they buy because of you. The difference between winning and losing is your follow up...

Follow up with them through email, text mes-sages, phone calls, face to face contacts, meetings, flyers, posters, whatever you can think of.

Got Mojo?

So how do you follow up without it becoming labor intensive? That leads us to...

Secret #3: Automated Follow Up

This is what we call "Automated Follow Up," which has been big for us. Instead of just following up with an email or video text message or video email, we'd now meet a prospect.

We'd send them video follow up either through email or text message and then we'd set up a meeting and then we'd follow up with them automatically.

And we wouldn't be just touching them one time; we'd have a video campaign of maybe 5 or 10 videos. Some of our clients have videos that go out for a year and a half, some even more so. This strategy worked well for both us and our clients.

Got Mojo?

Take Bill Montgomery. Bill Montgomery was running for the Maricopa County Attorney and he came to us with no database and no funding – plus, nobody knew who he was; he had no name recognition.

Bill's competition was Rick Romley. Rick had been in office for 16 years so he had plenty of funding and name recognition. People at the Arizona Republic knew about him and wrote about him. People laughed when Bill threw his hat in the ring because they thought a win was out of the question.

We went to bat for Bill. We preloaded videos. We had him follow up with the video just like we did whenever we met somebody.

He had four videos he preloaded. So if he met

somebody at a fundraiser, he would send a video.

If he met somebody at his office, he'd send another video.

If he met somebody at a community or public event, he'd send another video.

And if he met somebody in the media, he'd send another video.

All videos were preloaded and came with a long term follow up campaign that went out to people just educating them as to who he was, what he stood for, how he would drive people to the polls to vote and so on, and he did this all automatically using the "Mojo Matrix," our video relationship building software.

Got Mojo?

Bill built a relationship with every single person he met, while his competition was doing the same old things: road signs, flyers, pamphlets, etc. Bill was doing it differently and the results were abundantly clear. He got 75% of the vote. A stunning landslide upset. One of the biggest upsets in the last 20 years in AZ.

We helped Bill with a video to boost his campaign funding, so he was able to generate all these dollars to support his campaign and mobilize an entire community using video.

And all these people felt like they had a personal relationship with him because they got multiple videos over a period of almost a year. And at the polls, everybody showed up because they were in his corner every step of the way.

Got Mojo?

This is the power of video.

One video will trump thousands and thousands of emails. It's the next best thing to beaming yourself up, and it's extremely powerful because fear and skepticism are the enemies of marketing right now. When people see video, they see you; they know you; they like you; they trust you; and it evaporates all the fear.

Doing all of this over time is the secret weapon. It worked for Bill, it helped us win Marketer of the Year, and more importantly, it can work for you.

By now you might be thinking that we have the perfect system, but we had a problem -- we had meetings with people that weren't pre-motivated to buy, that weren't predisposed to buy.

Got Mojo?

We had plenty of meetings. Our calendars were completely booked. We are always full, but you want to -- you want to be able to know that if you're going to meet with somebody, they're ready to buy.

And second thing was that we were doing lots of one-on-one meetings, which for us was the best way to get customers, but we wanted the freedom to go to one or many.

We wanted to be on the line with tons of people and actually be able to sell lots of product to a lot of different customers, and actually be international so we wouldn't be confined to our own local region. This system is ideal for most of our clients for the same reason: being able to present on a very scalable basis so they can be in front of one or many. How can your competition compete with that? The truth is: they can't!

The problem was the overwhelm factor. We were working 80-hour weeks but not making as much revenue as we were looking for.

The meetings weren't the issue, they were coming fast and furious, but we didn't always do a lot of business because of the way our model was set up at the time. We were frustrated; we were overworked; we were overwhelmed; and we wanted to actually put a stop to this once and for all.

That's when we heard about this thing called a "webinar."

Got Mojo?

With a webinar you can share your knowledge with a mass audience. This was music to our ears.

We heard about our internet marketing friends out there that were making a lot of money doing these, and when I say a lot, I mean...well for example, one person made $300,000 in one webinar. Another made a $100,000. Another made $50,000. You get the idea.

As you might imagine we were skeptical in the beginning.

"Well, it's working for those guys, but will it really work for us?"

We weren't sure at first, but we were up for anything, since our options were dwindling fast.

Got Mojo?

And so we set out to put together our first webinar. It took us 30 days to put this webinar together, which is an eternity looking back on it now. In fact, there are some very simple and fast ways to do this, but I digress.

When we finally had it put together we were convinced we had a home run on our hands. So we got a registration page up; we drove traffic to it. And it was live.

At the end of the webinar we checked the sales numbers, and they were non-existent.

The webinar bombed big time!

To say we were disappointed would be an understatement. And it wasn't even about the money. I mean, imagine throwing this big bash and nobody shows up. That's how we felt.

Got Mojo?

So, after the brief pity party we went back into action: "All right, back to the drawing board."

We put together another webinar. We tweaked it, fine tuning this and that. It was the same webinar, we just finessed the content. We drove traffic to it. And would you believe it? That webinar we actually got one sale.

We were thrilled. I still remember that sale. What a rush.

We did another webinar and got four customers. And the webinars after that brought in up to 20 customers or more. We were excited and well on our way. Our persistence and focus paid off.

Last year we did over 100 live webinars in our quest to find the highest converting tactics. In a moment, we will show you how to use webinars for maximum profits and freedom without having to do any live webinars, a discovery that will save you countless hours.

As you might imagine, this leads us to...

Secret #4: Using Webinars To Sell To The Masses

Yes, webinars. They are no longer a secret, but in some circles they are like nuclear physics. People are clueless just how powerful these are or why they work so well.

The main reason is that it helps you build trust and rapport, and it helps you overcome objections in an instant.

For example, we have certain stages of our webinar where we are building rapport; we're introducing the content; we're talking about the clients we've worked with and so on. It's about building credibility, trust, and having them understand what your product or service really does. Clarity of your message is a must as a confused mind will not do anything.

We talk about the pain and big problems that people have. You must always connect them to their pain. There are two reasons why we do anything: 1) avoidance of pain or 2) gaining pleasure.

Then we talk about the solutions in a way that they can see it and almost touch it and taste it in their mind.

Then we make a compelling irresistible offer they can't so no to!

Got Mojo?

Instant gratification. Instant sales. Everyone was happy.

So now we have great response and lots of business, but there was a problem: too many leads.

You see, lots of people were registered, but the conversion on the webinars, especially live ones, was between 10% and 20%. Now don't get me wrong, this is very good for a webinar.

But what about the other 80% to 90%?

After all, they registered for the webinar. They must have been interested. In fact, we discovered that sometimes those people that didn't buy on the first round were actually very good clients as well.

But for whatever reason they didn't make that exact decision right then and there. The impulse buy was missing for this big chunk of leads. That's the expensive problem. That must be solved.

So we realized that we're burning up cash. We're throwing away money because we had all these leads and we weren't able to follow up with them and persuade them to buy.

This leads us to what we started doing next.

Secret #5: Maximizing Profits by Offering a Free Consultation

This is a huge one. A game-changer.

What we did was we started to offer a free consultation after the webinar.

Got Mojo?

And so now the missing piece of the puzzle had been found. Take a look:

- We drive people to the webinar.

- Prospect watches the webinar.

- We offer them a free consultation.

But strap yourself in because this gets even better. Here's the ninja thing that we did. This is what led us to both automate and free our lives, while giving us such a high closing ratio:

We had them schedule themselves into our calendar.

We didn't want them say, "I want a free consultation. Here's my information." Then you have to go back and forth with them, or you have to schedule it out or have an admin call them or send numerous emails so you come up with a time.

None of that! I repeat: We had them schedule themselves into our calendar.

And so, they'd go to our calendar and we had certain time slots they could pick out. They picked out the time slot that was right for them and voila! It was a beautiful thing.

And since we're doing this with people all over the world, I would simply show up on a conference line at whatever the time slot they picked out. Talk about leveraging and cloning yourself and your time.

The results were phenomenal. Up to 80% closing ratio on the first time we actually connected on the conference calls.

Got Mojo?

So instead of us chasing them, we slowed it down and put the ball in their court. This way, they pre-qualify themselves. If somebody has no money or can't make decisions or is only mildly interested, chances are they will not put themselves in your calendar and will not burn up an hour of your time.

This is a potent qualifying tool.

This is going to save you at least an hour to two hours a day at a minimum, and that's important because time is money. You can't buy back time. Saving one hour a day adds up to an eye popping six 40 hour work-weeks a

year. Imagine what you could do with that that type of time savings!

Got Mojo?

Not only that, but when these people are on the call, you can tell within the first 10 seconds of your conversation if they have watched the webinar. If they have, they are extremely excited and honored to talk with you and your team. They are extremely candid about their intentions, their challenges, their vision, and reveal exactly how to close the deal with them.

The webinar is a fear-removing, reservation-dissolving machine.

If your prospect is in fear, you could have a product or service that costs $1,000 and then drop the price to $50 and they still won't have the confidence to buy. The webinar takes away the fear and gives them the clarity they need. Now, they really understand who you are, what you're about, what your services are and what solutions you can give them. It's elegant in its simplicity.

It's like getting a great referral. No matter what you do or say, within reason, you can't screw it up. They're going to buy from you no matter what. That's what it feels like when these people go through this funnel and they get face to face with you or on the phone. They're ready to buy, and that's all there is to it.

We have many success stories with this model. People like Erin Babcock of Better Business Solutions, a credit card processing company.

From August of 2010 to August of 2011, he actually went up 500% in business using these very same systems. Powerful, eh?

Got Mojo?

So how did we make it so this system operates on autopilot?

That brings us to:

Secret #6: How to Automate Everything and Get Your Life Back

Here at Mojo we figured out how to automate everything. We came up with a funnel that would run in the background no matter what. That way people could watch your webinar any time that's convenient for them.

This means no more worrying about attendees, no more live call snafus, no more time zone issues, no more working around your schedule, no more stress of any kind. People come into your funnel; they've watched your webinar; they buy or sign up for a consult.

Got Mojo?

This method really allowed us to clone ourselves. As you can imagine, in the early days we were working like dogs -- upwards of 80 hours a week, and slaving away, not earning nearly as much money as we wanted to.

And now we're only getting on the phone with people that want to do business with us. It's a "set it and forget it" system. And the freedom that comes with this kind of system running for your company is just beyond words.

Remember one of the cardinal rules of marketing:

People love to buy but they hate to be sold.

Now, remember what we said earlier about building relationships. Today it's all about connection. Selling is out. Relationships are in.

Got Mojo?

With this system you're building solid relation-ships so that people will want to buy. It's that simple. Perhaps the best part is that you can do a lot of business with just a couple of custom-ers. With this system you will discover how to dial this up or dial this down as much as you want.

Got Mojo?

Chapter 4

Let's Do the Math

Let's look at it this way: the average entrepreneur is in front of two, maybe three people a week in an actual selling opportunity. That simply is not enough to have massive success.

We see that many people by noon on a typical Monday.

Now let's do the math. If you're in front of a couple of people a day, that comes to 10 people a week, which is 40 people a month. If you're face to face with 40 people or on a webinar or on calls in this selling situation, you're going to make a pile of money in this market. If you want to dial it up, there's a way to fill your funnels and we'll show you how to do all of that.

Got Mojo?

So by now we're starting to realize just what we have here. I mean, this really has massive potential. So much so that other gurus out there that were making tons of money on webinars -- and they were catching on that they were doing it all wrong.

They were missing out on the back end. They were missing out on so many more sales that they weren't capturing because they weren't implementing this kind of system. So, we put it together, tested it; tweaked it; and proven it over and over and over again in lots of different niches.

Why? Because we knew beyond all doubt that this was the key to our success. Let's go and see if this is the key to success for any other industries. So, we tested it in real estate, in other software companies, with social media marketing consultants, with local marketing consultants, with customers in over 70 industries. It works fabulously.

We'd have them enroll in a webinar, we'd send traffic to the webinar enrollment page and they watched the webinar.

Some people would buy automatically, which was great. But we would also get a certain percentage of people who would sign up for a strategy session, where we would then close 80%.

Wow!

Now let's say they didn't buy for whatever reason. Those people would go into a nurture campaign bucket for ongoing relationship building.

And as for those folks who didn't opt-in for the strategy session campaign?

Well, then we'd actually have a strategy session conversion campaign geared towards getting them to sign up and go to that strategy session opt-in page. That way, if they did opt-in, we have a reminder campaign just to put a bug in their ear about getting on that strategy session.

Now, let's say you have a sales team of 5, 10 or 20 people. When they get a prospect, no matter where the lead comes from, whether it's from the Internet, from your website, a referral, Facebook, it doesn't matter. Before that salesperson sits down with that individual, make sure that they watched this webinar.

This is especially powerful because it's like you have somebody doing a super bowl quality presentation that they will have experienced before your team sits down. And the advantage of this is you've answered all their questions in advance, but you have a consistent message from everybody.

Why is this important? Because if you have 10 people on the sales team, I can promise you there's maybe one or two people, if you're lucky, that are covering all the bases and not taking all the short cuts.

So now, you have the same message coming from everybody and your closing ratios go up.

Got Mojo?

The morale of everybody just explodes because they're making money and the company's making money. That's how you can use this on a large scale or a small scale. It doesn't matter the size of your company.

Once you implement this system into your business, you can literally drive all kinds of traffic to your offer. And if they opt-in for a free consultation, guess what? They still watch the webinar before they actually talk with you. So now, they're pre-qualified to meet up with you.

But here is the kicker. When you actually have this system working for you, you can drive unlimited amounts of offline or online traffic because we have mixes of both going toward the webinar enrollment page and our free consultation page.

Got Mojo?

So whether it's referral partners, affiliates or re-sellers, networking, trade shows or any other way you drive traffic to the webinar, you'll be sending them video follow-ups, driving them to your free consultation or your webinar.

The key here is to be constantly diligent from a marketing perspective. Have your free offers printed on your business cards, your flyers, your direct mail pieces, and any telemarketing you're doing.

So now you're not offering a chance to sell them, you're just offering them free content. This is the defining difference between winning and losing. Of course, if you're doing print, T.V., radio, etc. then send them to a webinar or a free consultation page. That's how you build a relationship to get them to purchase.

Got Mojo?

If you're doing social media, you can always send people off LinkedIn, Facebook, and Twitter to your webinar enrollment page.

If you're doing SEO, send them there. Pay Per Click Ads, press releases, even e-mail signatures. Direct them to your webinar enrollment page.

If you're doing blogging, direct them there. YouTube videos, podcasting, article writing, you name it. You can direct everything to your webinar enrollment page.

Conclusion

It All Starts Here

As you can probably tell by now, this is a game changing system and it can have massive implications on your business. But you probably have some lingering questions, which is why we want to talk with you one on one.

How to get a FREE consultation with us:

We're a real company with a team of 15 people here in Scottsdale, Arizona. We've got an actual brick and mortar office location.

We have some clients that paid us anywhere from $30,000 to $50,000 for consulting. And most of the stuff that we give them on a one-on-one is what's in our system and what we want to share with you in a free introductory consultation.

This is the time for massive action. Now is your time to take that first step.

We want to help you explode your business because this can be the time for you to reinvent your marketing. Success is all of our obligations. Really, it's our obligation to be successful, to reach our fullest potential.

This will change the way you do business. This will change your life. This will give you back time. And this will drop an enormous amount of money to the bottom line so you can really have a successful company and do many, many other things and give you back enormous amounts of time.

Got Mojo?

It all starts with the free call.

Want to view this book on video? Just go to:

www.MojoVideoMarketing.com/bookvideo

Get our free *Automated Webinar Selling System Overview* blueprints by going here:

http://mojovideomarketing.com/blueprint/Mojo-Webinar-Success-Blueprint.jpg

Go here to print off the *Mojo Traffic Formula*:

http://mojovideomarketing.com/blueprint/Mojo-Success-Traffic-Formula.jpg

Got Mojo?

Bonus Chapter

Mojo Matrix:

The Video Marketing Secret Weapon

At Mojo Video Marketing we're always on the lookout for the most effective, efficient way to get your videos out to the masses.

Entrepreneurs are on a constant search for the Next Big Thing, because when they have it before anyone else, it gives them an incredible competitive edge.

In the case of video marketing, everyone is jockeying for position. Everyone is trying to stand out from the crowd. Everyone wants to be unique and relevant.

But very few are accomplishing this, which is

why there are so many millions of videos out there that never get seen, no matter how great they are.

Now, imagine you could tell your story and sell your product or service in a way that is truly innovative, something that breaks new ground but has already been proven with dramatic results.

OK, we're getting ahead of ourselves here...

It's just hard to keep this under wraps much longer. ☺

First of all, I'd like you to imagine that you've just met somebody at a local function, a seminar or even an out of town event, and you want to follow up in a way that actually turns into something beneficial (as opposed to the usual results).

The old way is to formulate and send an email and cross your fingers.

But the new way is to actually speak to them again via video, which is a huge ice breaker, something they definitely weren't expecting. Who knows how many people they connected with at the same event, but it's your message that stands out.

Plus you can do all of this automatically, with hardly any learning curve at all, and your open rates will hover at around (are you sitting down?) 97%!

That's not a typo.

Here's what it looks like; let's log in and take a

peek:

OK you're looking at the Mojo Matrix back office.

Now, there's all kinds of very cool things that you can do in here from looking at your stats, creating email and video messages, uploading your videos, creating full campaigns, create

Got Mojo?

SMS, text message videos, import your contacts. It's just amazing all the things you can do.

Here's my favorite feature. It's called the two-click follow up. And all you have to do if you want – let's just say, you went out networking. You met somebody. Or you're just networking online. You want to follow up with them.

Got Mojo?

This is where most networking efforts fall down, because the follow up is a chore, so it just doesn't get done, despite the fact that it's a huge element to growing your business.

But this makes it a million times easier and more effective. In five seconds or less you can send the video email. Just pick out the first name, the last name, the phone number, the email address and BAM, you're done.

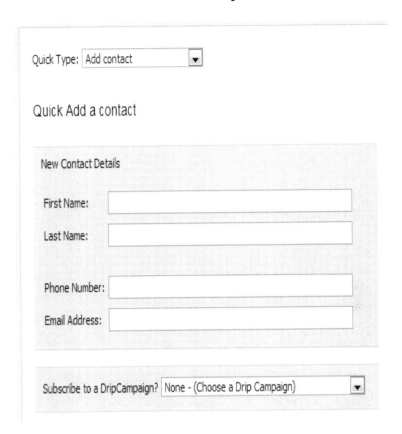

Then, when you choose the drip campaign, hit "Add this contact" and the video email flies out to your email inbox. And if you attach an SMS, that will go out, too.

Got Mojo?

And this is what it looks like in the email. And all you have to do is click on the "Play button" and it opens up the page:

hey Leah ,

You had to know we were going to do this,
but here's a quick video for you!

We think you'll totally love it =)
It's about our journey to Mojo Headquarters...
open video here

Let us know you got this!

--

Thank you,

Cory Sanchez & Ira Rosen

Got Mojo?

Now, if the contact reads it on their smart phone it will open up their video player in there too, because you can encode "mobile" when you set it up.

Now, feast your eyes on the calls to action, all of the links. And this is totally customizable so you can do whatever you want to this page.

Got Mojo?

You can change the color. You can change the logo. Add social media buttons, pictures, really spice up your branding. Anything and everything, and it's so turnkey, it's an entrepreneur's dream.

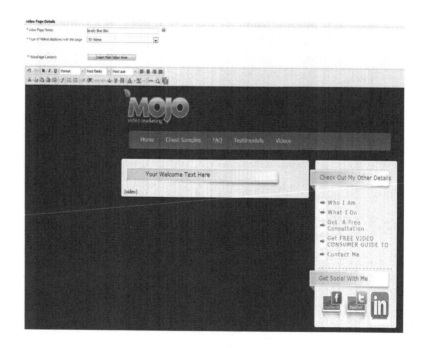

Got Mojo?

Here's what the campaign that we just sent looks like. You can see I have two messages going out immediately right here. One's an email and one's an SMS.

And then I have about five other videos that go out after that, and I can do whatever I want to those messages too. I can even have it go out at a pre-determined day and time, too.

Email Marketing Tip #5: Send your E-Mail campaigns Early to mid week before Lunch to get the best open rate, by this time you should be hitting them with an empty inbox.

View: All Drip Campaigns

Campaigns are emails or text messages that are sent to your contacts. Use campaigns to send campaigns, promotions, notification emails or responders.

Create a new Drip Campaign...

	Campaign Type	Medium Type	Attached Messages	Drip Campaign Name
☑	Drip Campaign	Email	1	july20
☑	Drip Campaign	Email	1	Ira - Follow Up

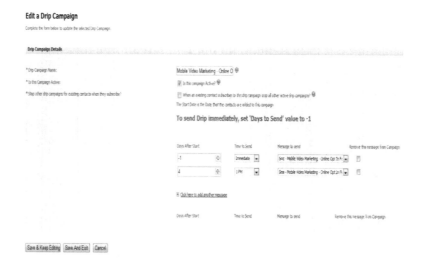

Now on the next page you'll see what a video SMS looks like in the Mojo Matrix. All I have to do is go over here to view all messages, pick one out and edit it, or you can start a new one, pick out the video you want and you're done. The video is inserted right into the message.

As far as tracking goes, the Matrix has that covered, too. Here's one of our campaigns. You can see it all laid out right here. You have the timeline of when the messages are being opened.

Got Mojo?

And here it is all color-coded. How many times was this video email opened up and by whom? And so, you can see over here. This one was opened 17 times, 11 times, nine, seven, seven, seven, and six.

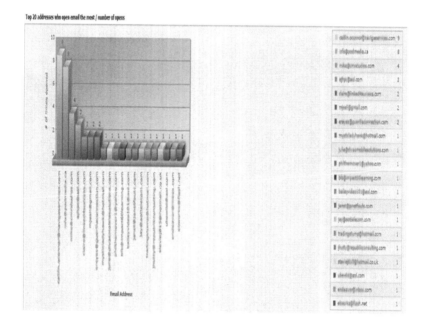

Effective marketing is all about testing and tracking, which is one reason why the Mojo Matrix is so cool. Let's face it, you can't manage if you don't measure.

Of course, we're just scratching the surface here. With Mojo Matrix software there are other amazing things you can do. For example, here you can see how to take those videos and embed them. Just click on the "embed" button and you get the code to embed the video. All you do is copy and paste it.

Got Mojo?

Here is what the popup code looks like to use the embed code for your video file.

Got Mojo?

The next thing you can do is import your con-tacts from a CSB, or just copy and paste the link here. You can create your list. You can manage your list. You can do all kinds of incredible things and make it push button simple.

Got Mojo?

The other thing you can do is actually watch what messages are going out. We created a number of drip video campaigns that run effortlessly and hands free, so you don't even have to manage it. As you can see above, we got about 360 pages of videos going out all for the next couple of months, all 20 deep.

So there you have it, the Mojo Matrix. As you can tell we're pretty proud of it over here at Mojo Video Marketing. But what's most exciting for us is the potential it has to explode your business.

You can grow exponentially when you put just a fraction of Mojo Matrix power behind your campaigns.

Testimonials

Here are just a few testimonials about Mojo Matrix:

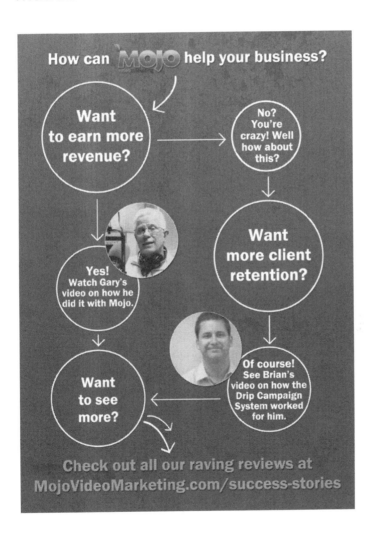

Got Mojo?

Brian North
Green Street Realty

"What's made this really, really simple for us is the Mojo Video Marketing team. From the innovative executives at the top all the way down to the video production crew, they've really held our hand and catered to us to the whole process."

Brian North

www.mojovideomarketing.com/brian

Got Mojo?

"Their staff, the ability to design a concept, to work with me and my style of communicating helped me to be successful.

And I'll tell you, whether you're trying to grow a new business or you're looking to communicate with a target audience of voters for a political campaign, Mojo Video Marketing could be the difference maker."

Bill Montgomery

www.mojovideomarketing.com/bill

Got Mojo?

I am delighted to work with Mojo. I chose them because I was looking to reposition our products and software. You are going to get specific results with them as they help you tell your story in a way that's compelling to others.

The whole staff have made me feel very comfortable, and I enjoyed working with them immensely.

Rodney Brim

www.mojovideomarketing.com/rodney

Got Mojo?

"I'll tell you right now. I -- I was flat broke in 2009, but because of my involvement with Mojo Videos, I was able to create just under $200,000 in profit in 2010. And in 2011, my best month was $23,000.

Now, you ask me if I'm going to recommend Mojo Video? That's like asking me am I going to stop drinking water. No! Because I love water and I love Mojo Video. And I'll recommend them to anybody."

Gary Lawrence

www.mojovideomarketing.com/gary

"...When I first signed up and we had sort of a mini marketing session and you guys gave me one tip that I used in my business that really made me thousands of dollars immediately.

I mean I used it and it worked in my business and I don't think you can get a better testimonial than that."

Debbie Bermont

www.mojovideomarketing.com/debbie

Got Mojo?

"We're now showing up on page 1 for some of our highly competitive keywords. Thank you very much!

We use your marketing suggestions to revamp our entire sales process, which -- which includes of course, videos. Check it out! We're using Green Screen now. Isn't that great?

As for our hot stuff, I just want to show you that. And we're getting great reviews. And we love that -- how we learned how to survey people on our list right now for new and future products to expand our product line to make more money."

Craig Sigl

www.mojovideomarketing.com/craig

Got Mojo?

Made in the USA
San Bernardino, CA
22 April 2014